This is where I say why I wrote it and dedicate the book to someone special. Well ok then.

I've been writing a long time. Middle school I guess. But I'm pretty shy. So I write. You will read that it's my anxiety keeps me this way. A blessing and a curse but I decided I should be heard. This book has love and lust also. My brain is such an amazing place I thought I should share my gift of creative writing.

I dedicate this book to You that bought the book. You believed in the book. And in Me.

My Family, I wouldn't trade any of you. Thank You.

The one who pushed and inspired and motivated me to finished the book.

I dedicate this book to Myself. I owe this to you for holding back out of fear for so long. This is just the beginning

I seem happier than most.

I put on a smile and use cute words.

Do for others not forgetting a uplifting quote.

But I'm broken.

Being held together by the piece of chewed gum I must have stepped in.

I hate it Here.

Here I mean my head.

Electrifying waves of thoughts racing around a circular track with no end in sight.

I'm dizzy.

Sick and I want off.

Tape holding on this side and If I pull it

I can jump.

But it's going to fast and that would hurt.

And Besides I'm already damaged.

Although what's a few scratches and bruises.

You won't notice the difference since I play healthy so well.

Best actress award goes to me.

Picture perfect on screen but standing in to big shoes behind the scenes.

Drowning in my blessings.

Death by abundance is what they will say.

And I did it with a smile.

It won't be to painful and definitely not loud.

I'll go in peace and this will be the only sound.

Because of you I learned how to write letters to God

When my world was upside down and couldn't spin

A pencil and paper

And I could find peace again

Your words on the page

mostly blue and always in script

wildly perfect cursive

written between His words

I learned

To pour my pain through my pencil and mail it secretly to Him

He heard me

He heard me like He heard you

And I learned

That the pain and sorrow is just my test so I grabbed my pencil

Writing down the answers I saw in your book

And not only the scripted passage left between the lines

but I learned to apply the printed text underlined and highlighted by you

I noticed your secret letters to God and pretended not to

But I learned to write those with my hands up and on bended knee

I've listened to you whisper your frustration and your joy

I've watched your tears run off your face and over your own words

They crossed right in front of me as I laid inside your arms

I liked to think I was comfort because you have always been my joy

White candle

Golden flame

I lite you in surrender

I come in pieces

Hoping for the heat to melt me back together

Stretched thin even inside the glass jar

Cold hard alone

A tiny spark makes an illuminating difference

A glow mimicking a mustard seed

Size and strength

Patience sways the flame

Catches my attention

It dance

Jumps

Reaching higher as it grows

Heat rises

Melting my pieces

Releasing the cold and out of place stiffness

Focusing on the golden wave

Breathing deeply the warmth

Feeling it blanket around me until

I'm liquid

I left my body is how to describe it

The vibrations I felt sent waves through me

I felt my aura expanding until I was

no longer in control

I let loose

I wanted it to last forever

I seen the ripples

The colors

Before and after floating away

Being lifted with a gentle pull of invisible hands

I was on top

Floating above watching my soul slip from my flesh

It was incredible

It was pleasure in all forms

I connected with the universe

And felt it's power

I can still feel it now

Pushing through my veins and surrounding me

I've gotten a taste before

A little here and there

Nothing like this time

Water flooded my body

Controlling the fire

The steam escaping felt like a light shining

Pushing through every pore

I was the goddess of love and passion

My root was activated by the alinement set up by the gods

Ascension was obtained that day

A new level unlocked

My Eye is open and connected to the rest

I see and feel and it's was the best

Happiness

And high vibrations

Mutually reached

I sing praises out loud

Thank you universe

Logic dissipates

Reality fazes

And I'm again lost in my own mind

Strapped into this roller coaster

of thoughts

Heart racing

Eyes closed

Speeding through each scenario

Trembling

Catching bits

and piecing it together

And as operator I can put a stop

to this madness

I just haven't quite yet mastered it

Nerves igniting in penetrating ripples, repeatedly

Last night I was touched by music and I can still feel it

Breathless

My body experienced total ecstasy

A starved request finally quenched during my last dying breath

(Exhales)

Now I am hooked

Each wave sends every part of me into unruly quivers

Intensifying and insisting to be felt

Divine Ascension was obtained without constraint

I'm captivated

Play it again

I need to feel

Pain or pleasure

Doesn't matter

this numbness is a bore

But where is the excitement

When is the party going to start

Set it on fire

Blow it up

Glass shatter

Blood dropping

Hot and stinging

I can feel it burning as it cuts deep

Dizzy with adrenaline

Shallow breathe

My eyes roll back

This is only skin deep and flesh only penetrates flesh.

My feelings

I thought were sharp as a knife but proved to be as weak as my knees when I am near you.

Standing against the walls you put up has turned in to a safe fortress but with no doors.

The single view provided by a tiny window

is of the white fence life that's replayed daily except without you.

A terrifying image on constant repeat my own private hell.

Locked away until you want me or forced to live separate from an "us" are my options.

Wishing for death after endless days of confusion

And so many why's

But Why?

A day without music

Have you ever thought about what it would be like to not hear?

No birds chirping singing an early morning song.

No whistle from the wind as it touches your cheek.

Could you imagine never hearing the church bells high in the air. Ringing on schedule

What about the rain drops racing to the ground.

Think of those songs that touch your heart and wipe it from memory. Sounds the beat makes never to be heard.

Could you not hear those tiny feet following your every move

Can you unhear the call of mommy?

I thought of the words and gave birth to music. But I don't want to share.

Shame on me

I haven't been kissed in the rain

But every time I hear the sound I remember what it..... almost felt like

Water from the heavens covered your hands that gripped my face pulling me closer to you

Today I heard the rain and it reminded me of you.

Watching droplets on your face that I am simultaneously blinded by

but finding myself preoccupied by something nearing my lips that I barely record the memory before my

attention quickly drifts

Temperatures rise with each fallen raindrop

Not sizzling but it felt that hot

Now I'm wet in more places than the rain has touched

You would think it was storming

just that much.

So come on

Kiss Me

Let's get this thing going

And It would've only been the beginning

Cause I had been waiting and waiting

I was so close when the rain

All of a sudden

Stopped.

Imagining what you're thinking

When I catch your eyes

Outlining curves

Stumbling on words

And Focus split

Images of possibilities

Positions

And places

Commence like the play button had been touched

but

without hands

Friction reaction initiated

Flames exposed

Stimulated

Guided by your eyes

and reciprocated

Lips don't move

Points are made

Boundaries pushed

And When we

Fuck

I see it in flashes of

Red

Hands to myself is so hard

Like your dick when I suck and sit on it

But ill touch myself

until

you can touch myself

Fingers walk on my lips

that don't talk

Understanding the language of

not just your tongue

Position after Position

Moans after screams

Followed by

I am Cumming for you Daddy

On Repeat

Until it's

Scratched

Nails on you back

Lips biting

snapping me

back to the physical

Just Daydreaming

Writer block is a bitch.

All I want to do is put my feelings on paper

It seems the only place I can trust my words will be kept secret

While outside of my head

But heart racing I still can't get it out

Shit just locked inside with all of my other

Crowded unfulfilled fuck of cluttered bullshit I feel is necessary to take up space.

Can't make out a complete thought due to the devastating fact

That each thought or idea gives life to its own worries and fears

Like bricks in a bag

Already overflowing and straps ready to snap

And in actuality I do not need to burst

Because I do fail to believe

it will be as quiet as this pencil on this fucking paper

Tonight. Tonight had to be a dream. But was it a fairytale or a nightmare?

There were forbidden touches as and spellbinding kisses that awoke a side of you and I that was forced to lie dormant until the night where the constellations aligned just right.

A night like tonight. A night where hands roam free and I see more than just the physical. It was Unreal? Or was it too real?

This fairytale is still being written but knowing the lustful actions that was performed in secret, how could those calculations ever add up to a happy ending.

Which makes me think this has to be a nightmare.

I mean how could so much excitement, fear and pure ecstasy be so wrong.

The way our bodies have been trying to fuse together just to feel whole.

Tongues intertwined during meaningful conversation stimulating every part of me.

I need a detour. More like a laps in time so I can indulge in the present just a little but not altering the future.

A back to the future kind of moment where only you and I can remember and cherish the time that doesn't exist.

An alternate universe that only revealed by the touch of your lips. A place where my Yoni juices flow like rain on a summer night.

So our touches can be enjoy without judgment and fear.

With time to connect as one mentally and physically. A private Oasis within our own reality.

Don't wake me. Let me live this dream at least for

Tonight

Staring at the stars

Looking around for God

Thinking if only I could lasso the moon

I'd get a better view

I just want to talk face-to-face

to ask the question why

and then listen

Maybe even what or how for a better understanding

A little clarification to sort out this confusion

With some instruction from the inventor

I'm sure can do it

Myself

I had an affair with music.

OMG I know.

How could I bring someone else into what we have for years?

I am horrible!

I let it go on behind your back.

Lying to your face each time.

But each time I hear the melody.

The time spent with music, no pencil to hold, paper to find.

It's simple with music.

The Rhythm Is there.

Each note matched and tested during the Big Show.

But my words.

My words dance with each chord, embracing them with the deepest tones.

I fell for music.

Music connected my words

Amplifying their meanings and changing my world.

I can't live without music.

The electric vibe and Award-winning sound

Let's give music a round of applause

Music has touched all of us I'm sure

But that is only the beginning of

My Music and Me

I get disappointed every time there's

another crack in this childish make believe I assumed would last

Gazing upon you without a crown on your head.

I shake mine.

No. Prince Charming is not who I am searching for

That's the same lame ass that was with Cinderella, Beauty and probably Ariel too

I want the Beast

He gave her a library before he touched your body.

Just Think

Standing in line to get a moment with Everyone's prince

Give me the Wolf

He'll learn my ins and outs

Know my scent like no other.

Take his time

But not afraid to pounce

Let Snow have all 7

That shit won't get her into heaven

Give me My King.

One I can worship because he knows God is a woman

Now step aside

and clear his path

To My Daughter's with Love

I see you in all your glory

Angels sang for you the day you were born

The most angelic creature God herself personally designed

Eyes like almonds

Brown but shiny as if you were hiding diamonds behind them

A girl's best friend

Bronze Melanated skin

Like the richest Egyptian Goddess

Sun charged curls reaching out

Making it hard to keep your Crown straight

But royalty nevertheless

Commanding a room like a true leader

Yet you haven't said a solitary word Intelligent and articulate conversation spoken through full lips

Naturally tinted cheeks

Perfectly arched eyebrows

No make-up on

Model tall, Model fine

Way before your time

So grow slow

Learn you

And Love you like I do

Let me be

I'm fine being me.

Why worry about me?

The only person with the problem is....... Well it ain't me.

Let Me Be

My Weird is awesome it's the best about me and makes me ME

And who else would I rather be

I'm fine being me

I've gotten to know me

Although complex, yet wasn't the art of Picasso an eye addicting maze

Behold the mess that is me

and let me be

I'm proud of me

aren't you?

You know Proud of you? Could be why I'm fine being me

 so let me be me

 and you.

Well

go be you

I miss Me

The Me before I cut my hair

The Me that thought a new do would ease the change

I miss the Me

I used to be carefree Me

Me who flowed with the wind

Shined with the sun

And dance under the moon

I miss that Me

The one who knew

Me

The one who could see

Me

The one who loved

Me

You know Me Me

I miss her

Find her

In ME

When they ask tell them I wanted to die.

Tell them the pain I feel became to much to handle.

I bare it alone and others on top.

With no help and strength fading I suffocated in view of all.

Watching me weaken with excitement and aww.

Still no assistants just watching me go.

Placing bets on when or how from each bystander and friend

yet still no hand to help me fend.

I rather leave this pain behind.

The darkness ahead is what I welcome.

No audience or pointed fingers

Just my mistakes and me.

Silence

Just A Rib

In a crowded room

With you by my side

Noticed by everyone but you.

Your eyes show emptiness your touch so cold

Alone and invisible next to you.

It's killing me to be with you but your heaven is where I'm trying to be

Not until something goes wrong and never right do you pay me some attention

And not the only woman in the room,

I just want to feel your body against mine kind of whispers in my ear

But the how could you let this happen it's all your fault kind of insults

That turns my invisibility into naked in front of the class

That makes me wish to be again unseen.

My heart skips a beat as I become a failing god for a spoiled village in your eyes.

Afraid of the secret crucifixion that occurs daily with just your voice.

Dying inside only to be lifted briefly by the hope I blindly carry for us.

Too much of me is wrapped in you.

Constantly thinking I can be good for you and good to you.

You can be my one and only.

You can be all that I need.

See look you can breathe for me.

Oh wait!

I'm invisible you can't even see me.

Loving you was easy

finding a reason not to want you is going to be the death of me

but I think I should at least try

Inside of my mind is where this fantasy of you live so comfy and cozy

because of the burning desire to be your perfect match.

But it's crazy.

I love you and you don't even know I'm here.

Maybe I wasn't in love with you. I mean I am doing so well with you gone. My eyes are open and mind is clear. I can see more than just my next 10 steps I can even see your. I may have to go to the store sometimes twice in one day because I am remembering so well everything on the list in my hand. People notice a great change in me. The way I flipped out again for nothing on another undeserved stranger. I started to enjoy being without you so much because I got to stay in bed staring at my phone.........For Hours! Yes hours that's if I wasn't sleep of course. Napping. More like hiding under my covers and watching my phone. I was even trying to read this Really interesting book. Wow it was so good. Well except for the romance part. Were the man is there and the woman wants him there and he promises not to leave her but you know some where down the pages he does. Even if they say I Do. Yuck! So I skip those. Which makes it hard and nothing makes sense. But since that's not the case with me. I am good with the sunshine on my face. Shining bright, glasses on 24/7. Although this eye sweat is beginning to bother me. Constantly wiping but people assume they are tears of joy. Lol No. Its probably my allergies again for like the hundred time. And don't let someone mention you, it just makes me want to scream but the eye sweat or allergies make it a little difficult to let the tiniest sound out. Which is ok because who knows what artistic twist of appellation of you would emerge out of the expressions my heart and mind have developed for you. So move on as I have done. Continue not to worry. I am doing blissfully benighted as you can see.

I've forgotten how a pencil feels in my hand.

The coldness of the empty pages.

I could find reason to blame others.

Like technology or time

but time is there as soon as I buy a notebook and pencil.

I miss the words flowing mindlessly from my hand through the #2 onto the page.

Not harder than finding the next letter on this tiny key board (backspace) .

A freshly sharpened point,

the sound,

it makes that white noise kind of soothing sound.

I can focus.

I can see my words on the lines even before my pencil puts them there.

I miss that feeling.

The feeling of holding my notebook when I was done

like the way a best-selling author hugs her manuscript fresh off the printer

still warm and ink slightly wet.

Knowing its greatness before it hit the shelves.

My pencil completes me.

It was the tool I should have been born with.

A true extension of me

Inhale

I just want to scream I hate you but I can't

I fell for you and now I'm all

choked up on words trying to leave you.

I miss you

Your not mine but I wanna kiss you

Dirty little secret that's the issue

Deep breathes Eye sweats

I'll get over it. No regrets

Passion feels different when it's real

Pray you won't forget The feel

Your touch

I can't

Exhale

Inhale

And still I wanna be selfish and possessive

Even if your not mine

I didn't mind sharing

But not this time

Like abracadabra

2 snaps and a kiss

Blow out this candle

Close my eyes and

Magic

Not a wish

My power to great

Luck and love is my air

My manifestations always appear

Not envy maybe lust

Blind eyes can't fuss

So stop looking outside

And focus on you

Cause I'm not sure what

my demons will do

(Inhale, Exhale)

Patience is a killer

silent but deadly

high pressure

pressure I want to feel around me and inside of me

I can't wait no more

I can't be away from you

enjoying every sneaky moment

keeping it only between us 2

but 3 is company

and I love a dope party

putting my lips to you inhaling every hit of you

kissing you is everything

the mood take over peace satisfaction calm I just need a quick taste

its better when no one knows but I really don't care so here it goes

I need to hit this blunt

It's a delicacy that my tongue begs for and won't settle for.

So I keep tasting.

Putting my lips to a little bit of......well everything.

No time to question the cook.

I'm starving!

Feeling weak for what I hunger.

This unfulfilled craving likes nothing.

I've drank from all the cups and ate from every plate.

Each although delicious at first bite left a bitter taste and my stomach turned.

Oh how much of me will waste away.

I can't keep it together

Letting my mind wonder on the wonders

that my other 5 senses haven't had the pleasure of experiencing.

Even though the 3rd eye has spotted it in a dream of another

and have my eyes trying to behold your beauty

with or without the lights on.

The taste was recognized by a tongue that has only heard of you.

Yet this emptiness have supplied me with enough will to discover the cure for this appetite.

 You.

I forgot how much this depression hurts

1st it's the wrong amount of sleep

Sleeping too much

Sleeping too little

Even sleeping bad

My chakras start to misaligned

Head gets cloudy

I went from multitasking several lives to scheduling brushing my teeth

My heart hurts

Its beating irregular in my throat

I can't breathe

I can't talk

Not only are my words tongue tied

My thoughts are completely backed up

Not to much different from my stomach issues

Hungry but not hungry and Knots in my stomach

Aches and pains wrapped around my body

Hugging me so tight lessening the oxygen my system is trying

to hold on to

But it's the only embrace that has held this long and with familiar pains

I don't resist

I let it consume

Before I know it I'm sleeping in the arms of my pain

Cuddling sorrow

Tears come and go

Some with reason most without

But it for the moment helps

Then 3-2-1

It hits me again

Knocking me off my feet

Ungrounded in an instance

Completely off balance

Deep breath of relief

Until I see where I've landed

"I've got to get out" on repeat

Then Reality!

It's all on me

I panic!

Heart race

Shallow breaths bring body sweats

Pulse so strong from all the blood racing around

That drunk dizzy feeling

Looking up

While I'm 6ft down

Breathe! Stay with me. Please don't leave me.
Open your eyes. Please!
Standing here watching your life flash before my eyes. 6 short years is all
you were given. But I need more. Come on breathe look at me don't go.
God made me but you built me
I can't do this without you
pinky promised I wouldn't leave.
That promise won't be broken. But it can't work without you.
Weak and struggling to breathe I feel hopeless.
Do something Doc.
Do something. Please I can't lose my baby.
It's not supposed to happen this way.
Mama is here I repeated mama is here.
Help is coming I pray.
Holding you close tiny and frail.
I give you my life cause you are my life.
Feeling hope fade like your heartbeat.
Beep beep beeeeep.
I feel my body dissolve into the floor the cold tiles
I just lay there adrenaline gone
energy depleted
eyes swollen and red
I become inconsolable with each mention of your name
I wish I could breathe.
No strength to stand.
Words have no meaning no taste for food.
I wanted to give up I wanted to find you there.
That there I couldn't go yet.
Not that I didn't try.
My master plan included you and
never imagined doing this alone
but A promise is a promise
and I must breathe until I see you again

What's wrong with me?

I'm a writer who doesn't write

a few poems here and there

wrote one book

But started several

and even that child's play could be better

I'm My Own Worst Enemy

I'm a shooter without a gun

A racer with a..... minivan ?

I find myself searching for a muse when I should be staring into a mirror

Lost on my own creative journey

Blinded by my own submission

But I haven't given up.

I'm scared but I'm afraid to tell you.

Trembling

Eyes extra wet trying to keep any tears from falling

Because then

Then you'd know

That my anxiety it at its highest and doubt is

sitting in my throat choking me

Not a heart attack but my chest hurts

I

can't

catch

my

breath

Scared to die

But this isn't death

This is my cost of living

I'm supposed to be able to bare it

but I can

hardly stand on my own

Pretending I'm strong

So you don't look down on me

Condemning me

Pointing out the weakness I can't control

And Blink

My smile is back

Painted across my face

Like an over worked clown at the end of the party

So I hope your happy

Same show different day

Thanks and come again

About the Author

Energy… You have it.

That it. You mold it.

You are, It.

Sunlight through the blinds on a Sunday morning.

Can't hide this light…

The parties liven up when you arrive

The wine tastes sweeter whenever we toast.

They miss you when you leave.

They wow at your work. If you touch it, it changes.

Purposeful pen. Delicate thoughts. Words of intention.

Yea you got it, But you share it.

Its infectious. Irreplaceable. Necessary.

Protector of the divine feminine. Protect her.

Full moon magic or Summer Sunlight the results are clear,

everything will go according to plan as long as you're here.

My dearest and deepest most articulated expressions hardly live up to the expectations that your presence brings.

So much value. Yet no amount will suffice.

So much potential realized.

I know why these thoughts won't fade and it's so easy to recall.

It's because I'm STILL THINKING.